SALES -
Something Out Of Nothing

SALES –
Something Out Of Nothing

Frank Siebert

authorHOUSE®

AuthorHouse™
1663 Liberty Drive
Bloomington, IN 47403
www.authorhouse.com
Phone: 1-800-839-8640

Published by AuthorHouse   04/10/2013

ISBN: 978-1-4817-3909-2 (sc)
ISBN: 978-1-4817-3918-4 (e)

Library of Congress Control Number: 2013906622

Working in sales provides you with a rewarding career that is full of excitement. Whether you are just starting out or want to better your skills in your current career, I am happy to welcome you as an asset to my team. In these pages, I will try to instill in you useful information that will build on your skills as a salesperson.

Everyone has their own learning method and speed with which they are the most comfortable. I would like to show you the ways that I have found my success in hopes that you can get useful skills to add to your set of sales tactics that already work for you. As a salesperson, I try to create excitement in the customer for making the purchase rather than directly requesting that the customer commit to buy whatever product I am selling.

The most important concept for you to take away from my teaching is the importance of humility in the sales role and the idea of giving the customer the power to tell you what he or she wants. Keep in mind that you are responsible for wisely directing the customer's focus so they want to buy.

So, without further ado, let's begin . . .

SALESPEOPLE

As a group of new professionals, we must always come up with creative solutions for ways to improve upon our sales practices in order to get the desired sale. With every completed sale, we feel the pleasure that comes along with the financial benefits of landing a deal. We will not get this feeling without first having put in the needed effort and cleverness that brings about a sale. We must start with the proper education and training.

No matter what you are selling, you will benefit by learning the specifics of the product or service you are offering to your customers. Develop a complete understanding of what is available through your company's rivals, and make sure you can convince your clients that your products are better. No one wants to deal with a salesperson who cannot answer any important questions about their product. It is especially off-putting to a client when a salesperson is clearly being dishonest to make the sale. Do not misjudge your customers and always go into a sale assuming they are shrewd, informed people. It is not only poor policy to take advantage of inexperienced customers. It is also morally questionable and it will likely lead to problems for a company down the road. Salespeople only hurt themselves in the long run by causing distrust. Because of the poor reputation of some people who work in sales, many customers are instantly distrustful of anyone in a sales role. Understand this and take it into account when dealing with your customers. You must try to bring back trust in clients who have been taken advantage of in the past. Customers who grow to trust you in this way are likely to return for future business and might spread the word about your honesty and fairness. **Giving people the products they need at a fair price, maintaining honor and trust in your dealings, and giving the highest-quality service to customers who see your real concern** are some of the basics of sales work.

Consumers Price Point

I have noticed in my experience with sales that each consumer seems to have a certain price that they are willing to pay for a given product or service.

Often customers will alter this price slightly if they think that it is in their best interest to do so. As a salesperson, you must first find what this price is and decide if you can offer the product at that price. If so, your job is easy and your customer will be happy with the purchase.

However, the method of selling that I want to use is more effective and creates a stronger feeling in the minds of customers. I like to teach fellow salespeople to show customers that they are giving exactly what the customer wants for less than he or she was planning to pay. In this way, customers leave with the feeling that they have really profited from the sale. The salesperson appears to these customers to be at the top of their field, and customers come back for more business and give the salesperson/company repeated referrals. This kind of service shows a level of creativity and effort that is unmatched by competitors and is an important key to a salesperson's ability to regularly close sales.

FINDING THAT PERFECT NUMBER

The most common sales strategy is to cheerfully begin with a high number and work with the customer until a number is found that the customer is willing to pay. Some sellers openly ask customers how much they are willing to spend. At times, these methods may work with success, but more often than not they merely prove offensive to customers. Methods like these are thought of and used by a salesperson looking only from their point of view in the exchange rather than seeing what the customer wants. For this reason, a salesperson tends to struggle when using these methods. I will describe below what I have found to work better than these traditional methods.

First, go into the exchange thinking of the consumer as a personal friend. Work to **appear genuine** in everything you say and in all of your gestures. Offer them refreshments and do everything you can to make them feel comfortable. Be creative. If you take the time to be courteous and respectful to your customers they will, in turn, feel compelled to show you the same courtesy. Subconsciously, the customer is already feeling a connection with you and you know you have their attention. In sales, first impressions are important. The very beginning of your encounters with customers is an important part of winning them over. After the initial greeting and the presentation of the product, it is of vital importance to **give your customers some space**. Customers will be repelled by a salesperson who is too "clingy" and who is constantly crowding them. Give your customers time to think about options and simply observe enough so that you are aware of any expressions they make that may indicate a need for assistance or an unanswered question. Typically, a customer with a question will be glancing around inquiringly. Skills at watching people's body language are important in sales, and you want to try to get a good look at your clients before speaking to them. (Once, I mistakenly asked a man with a prosthetic arm if he needed a hand. He responded, "As a matter of fact I do!" I felt awkward and embarrassed.)

When you are at the point of answering customer's inquiry, be sure to **listen to their words carefully**. Whether they are looking for a different product, have a question about your services, or are ready to make a purchase, pay attention and focus on every word they say. You need to be able to quickly devise a solution that will meet their needs. (Remember not to be too eager to discuss a price, but rather try to provide information on the many benefits of a given product before discussing the product's dollar value.) Show the consumer all products that relate to their needs or inquiry. (Try not to always bring the consumer to the most expensive product, as many salespeople would do, because this often discourages consumers from dealing with you.) Avoid bringing up items that the consumer has not expressed an interest in unless they give you some sort of sign that they might be interested. After you show them the product or products that they have mentioned, provide them with important information on any alternatives. You can, perhaps, mention a product with a different price or, perhaps, a higher quality item. Listen to the customer's input and respond to the issues they mention. Showing customers less expensive items first is important to **building trust**. If you are bringing cost-effective items into the conversation, customers will know that you are not pressuring them or trying to up sell them. Customers will be more likely to reject more expensive products if you appear to be pushing them towards such products.

You have now taken the steps necessary to make your customer feel confident in your genuine desire to provide assistance without trying to up sell or manipulate their decision. Understanding that you need to find that special number your customer is willing to pay, you can begin to question your customer regarding price expectations. Please let it be clear that trust is not to be used as a tool to take advantage of the customer. Rather, trust is established in the exchange so that the customer can make an informed decision based on the information you have given.

Since you have now established your credibility in the mind of the consumer, you can now be much more open about aspects of the sale that you were, at first, reluctant to discuss. While **being conscious of what is truly best for the customers**, you can now begin to work towards closing the sale. The question that you should be asking is, "How can I complete the sale when I'm still not sure what the customer is expecting to pay?" Keep reading for a solution to this problem.

During the first part of our contact with the customer, we offered information on all of the products relevant to their needs. We were constantly polite and genuine in our mannerisms, and we did not crowd nor pressure the customer. We always **put the customer's best interests first**. (The elusive number is this . . . .) **The consumer will be able to choose his or her price after YOU (the salesperson) have educated them** with the appropriate information. In this way, you have created the elusive number. The special number that your customer is willing to pay is determined by how you educate your consumer and how your interaction with the consumer affects the **"perceived value"** of the product or service you are dealing with. When this process is carried out in the correct way, the consumer will spend the amount that they are comfortable with and they will be happy with your expert assistance.

Congratulations!

Now that you have finished the first part of learning how to become highly effective in a sales role, it is up to you to use these first few lessons when working with customers. It could take some time before you feel perfectly comfortable putting these ideas into effect, but one way you can measure your success is by considering how much you are **enjoying the sales process**. As you progress, you will notice a rise in confidence and ease in your dealings with customers, and you will see how the doors to continued sales opportunities open. Simply give customers what they need and want and you will see the results. This not only makes us good salespeople, but **brings us a feeling of happiness, self-worth, and contentment**. The sale itself is really only a part of **expressing genuine concern for your customers**.

Think about what has been discussed up to this point. I have put some words in bold print to emphasize them and to allow you to reference them quickly while looking over this guide again in the future. These important phrases include:

(When you read these words, absorb their meaning emotionally and consider how they relate to the sales process . . .)

- **Appear genuine.**
- **Give your customers some space.**
- **Listen to the customer's words carefully.**
- **Put the customer's best interests first.**
- **Build trust.**
- **Do what is best for the consumer.**
- **The reward for putting the consumer's needs ahead of our own is happiness, self-worth, and contentment.**
- **Enjoy the process.**

Now I'd like you to read the words over again and apply them to how you would treat someone you love . . .

You have a lot to work on if **any** of these words bring **different emotions** to you when applied in different ways. This is the **most important part of working in sales that I can teach you**. If you learn nothing else from reading these words, I want you to remember the importance of feeling these concepts emotionally, in the context of working as a salesperson. **Love and compassion for your customers will allow you to perform well in every interaction.** It is a shame that emotions are pushed to the side in the business world when they are a vitally important part of all sorts of human interactions.

If you find yourself wondering what all this has to do with sales, trust me. This sort of understanding has everything to do with sales. Let me provide an example.

When did you last **deceive** someone who is important to you?

- How did you feel afterwards?
- Is this a behavior you would repeat?
- What if no one would find out?
- Do you see the connections I am trying to make?

Even if you do not have a particularly close relationship with someone—even if you are detached enough from someone that there is no way they would ever know—it is never okay to deceive or bend the truth. You should not be selling a product if you cannot sell it without stretching or modifying the truth. It's good to go by this rule: If you would feel guilty doing something to someone you care about, you shouldn't be doing it to anyone else.

Yes, it's strange to consider this in terms of sales strategies . . .

However, you wouldn't believe how many salespeople remain ignorant of this basic principle when they are in the process of working towards a sale with a customer. Honesty is ALWAYS the best policy, in every situation. I cannot put enough stress on this idea.

I would like to share a story from my sales experience that really cemented in my mind the importance of honesty in salesperson/client relations.

I had a client who wished to purchase a product that she was very much intent on buying. The sale was worth $10,000 and I would have earned $1,200 on it in commission. It was perfect in every way for her—the right color, sufficient durability, it was on sale, and it was the last one left. She was so certain of the purchase that she gave me the deposit right away. Two days beforehand, the vendor of the product had notified everyone working in selling that product that there were major problems and the product would not, in fact, last. They informed us that the manufacturer's warranty would be void on all sales from that day onward.

This left me in a sticky predicament. I had a few days to think about the situation because she had told me that she would be back to pay the balance on the purchase. I could sell her the product, take my commission, and let her enjoy the product until she discovered the malfunction. If she tried to return the item, I could simply let her know that the manufacturer would no longer honor the warranty on the product. I could make it look like I had no way of knowing beforehand about the product's problems. She would never know the truth. My other option was to inform her of the issues with the product and allow her to choose from among the alternatives.

How do you think you would have handled the situation?

In the end, I decided to let the customer know about the situation with the product's flaw and the manufacturer's warranty even though it might have a negative impact on my income. However, before contacting the customer, I did a bit of research and located a product that was similar but more expensive. I then called her at home and left a message explaining the situation. I didn't receive a response before my weekend off, so I asked one of my colleagues to let her know I was off if she happened to stop by.

When I returned to work the next week, I found an envelope on my desk that was from this customer. It read:

Dear Mr. Siebert,

I wanted to take this opportunity to express my deepest gratitude. My husband recently passed away and he left me some money to purchase a gift for myself that he could not afford to give me while he was alive. It would have broken my heart had I purchased something that would not have lasted. You have no idea what this means to me. I cannot thank you enough for your honesty!

Sincerely,

Jane Doe

Enclosed with the letter were two tickets to a professional sporting event that I was very eager to attend!

Right then I realized the full severity of the situation. Immediately, I felt like a terrible person for having considered the possibility of selling this customer a defective product for my own financial gain. This individual had just lost her husband and she wanted to be able to remember him for years to come by the product that she had sought my assistance to purchase.

This event more than any other really changed the way I saw the value of honest conduct in my sales career. I had really never thought very much about the feelings of my customers and had, instead, focused on landing sales at all costs. I looked back at my previous instances of selfishness and felt quite guilty. Yet this guilt was a good thing, for it had made me come forward with the truth. Had I not been honest, I would have had a much more negative impact on her life than I could have imagined. Now, I no longer sell as I did before. Ever since this incident I have stuck to a vow to never take for granted the power of honesty! The reason I am telling you about this is because I would like it to be apparent to you that . . .

You never know the reasons behind a customer's purchase and you never know where the money is coming from to make that purchase. You should always keep in mind the significance of a purchase in the mind of a customer. Working as a salesperson is not about landing a sale and making money, but instead it's about fulfilling wishes and catering to the needs of customers to whom you show the highest level of respect and professionalism.

PREPARING THE CONSUMERS

We have just seen that anyone is able to sell a product—even an inferior product. The sad truth is that many people would have gone ahead with the sale to "Jane Doe" without paying it much thought. Preparing your customer for interactions with such salespeople is our next important task in being dedicated professionals in the sales field. Salespeople can resort to a variety of different "styles" in order to close a sale. The following is a list of a few such styles.

The "Tell the client what he/she wants to hear" style. This is one of the most dangerous of styles among salespeople. The unknowing customer will examine a product and the salesperson will ask them a series of questions, but not with the intent of informing. This type of salesperson will ask questions with the intent of tricking the customer regarding the product's quality or worth. The consumer receives only positive information regarding the product's characteristics, and proceeds to purchase the product. This, more often than not, results in disappointment for the consumer when the product does not live up to the salesperson's description.

The "I am the ultimate authority on this product and everything else" style. While these salespeople may have the experience, they don't have the heart. They feel superior to the consumer due to their knowledge about the product and they, basically, bully the consumer trying to belittle him or her. Needless to say, many consumers feel intimidated by this behavior and they often finish encounters with such salespeople feeling foolish. Often, the pressure inflicted by this type of salesperson pushes a consumer to buy a product just to end the encounter as quickly as possible.

The "Please buy this product from a poor, desperate person trying to scrape by" style. A salesperson using this approach looks out for consumers who seem a little too nice. They prey on any softness in a consumer and will go to any lengths to get the consumer to sympathize with them. They will make consumers uncomfortable by giving out too many details of their personal lives and exaggerating about how hard they must work when making their living on nothing but commission. While shameless, this tactic can be very effective on kind, well-meaning consumers who don't know how else to respond, other than to shell out money to keep the desperate salesperson afloat financially.

The "Let's buy it now, now, now!" style. This is perhaps the most stereotypical of all sales approaches. Pushy, assertive salespeople constantly insist on finishing the sale as soon as possible. They don't care about working out all the details or seeing to it that all the right information is shared. They are not very concerned with answering consumer questions and they only answer questions by circling back around to the prospect of a speedy purchase. They are not at all interested in learning about the consumer or getting to know them. They often succeed in rushing a consumer into an unwanted purchase.

How many of these "styles" have you seen in your dealings with salespeople? How did you feel when these styles were being used on you? Did you fall for the traps or did you leave the store without making a purchase? You might even have seen other styles in the salespeople you have come across. The whole point of bringing up these various styles is to emphasize that **constant pressure** is basically considered a defining characteristic of a salesperson these days. **ALL** of these tactics center around various forms of pressure.

So, how can you prepare your consumers for these tactics and see to it that the consumers you deal with quickly learn to flee from salespeople who show these behaviors? Well, first of all, show them the exact opposite of pressure. Release! Yes, release. We must provide an outlet of release and comfort for our consumers. We must offer that refreshing calm amidst all of the sales hype and noise.

How do we do that? We use the ideas that have already been mentioned before: **appear genuine, give your customers some space, listen to their words carefully, put the customer's best interests first, build trust, and do what is best for the consumer**. In comparing this method of sales to the various "styles" we've discussed, do you immediately see the difference? For a consumer, a salesperson who tries to appear genuine and concerned is like a diamond in the rough to the typical consumer who is accustomed to the senseless noise of the common pressure mongers who traditionally work in sales. You will be surprised at how much you will stick out in the minds of your consumers compared to other salespeople they have dealt with. This method is what provides you with boundless opportunity in the world of sales. Step by step instructions are the best way to teach a process, and this is what I want to provide for you. Let me give you an example.

Mr. and Mrs. Smith enter a showroom. They would like to purchase a washer and dryer for their home. You should assume that clients coming to do business with you have already looked around a bit and have dealt with salespeople elsewhere prior to meeting you. When you have arrived with the customers at the area where the product is displayed, you ask (in a courteous tone) if they have any questions or if they would like some time to look around on their own.

They tell you that they would like some time to browse, and so you take a small step back and respond, "Not a problem, I am just going to be over here and I will check back on you shortly." After saying this, you give them time and space to get an idea of the choices. After a few minutes have gone by, Mrs. Smith shows body language that means she has a question, so you approach once again. From a distance (about a car's length away), you ask if they have a question. Mrs. Smith would like to know if you have any front loading models that stack because this type of appliance is smaller and frees up space. In response, you lead the couple to the most **inexpensive** model that fits their description and say the following, "This model is our most affordable front load washer and dryer set. What features are important to you?" While Mrs. Smith answers, listen intently and look into her eyes. Nod when you agree with something she says (*all the while staying at least an arm's length away*) and try to match her body language.

After her answer, explain how important certain features are and which features are not very useful or unnecessary. (*This is of vital importance! She might not yet be aware of it, but due to your honesty, you have just made her question every other salesperson she has already talked to or will talk to in the future. Salespeople rarely say anything negative about their products, and because you have just revealed a weakness in a product you are trying to sell, there is a bit of doubt or unfamiliarity in her mind. She's asking herself, "What aren't the other salespeople telling me?"*)

Now, bring her to the next item that fits her specifications but that has a slightly higher price. Again, listen to her comments on the product. Answer any questions that arise and make a point of saying with genuine sincerity that you don't want her to feel pressured in any way about making a purchase. You want her to understand the importance of not buying a product with which she is not comfortable. No one wants to feel pressured when they are trying to make an important decision and you want Mrs. Smith to know that you understand this. (*This statement gives the consumer the understanding that it is wrong for someone to be pressuring them, and they should not ever feel pressured when making a decision regarding a major purchase. Now—if and when the customers leave to look at other stores—they will have my words in the forefront of their minds. They will have their guard up when another salesperson pressures them.*)

The next thing to do is bring them to the most expensive product. Explain the features and benefits, but also shed some light on both the pros *AND* the cons of the more expensive product. Mrs. Smith absolutely loves it but it is out of the couple's price range. You could say something like this, "Although most salespeople would tell you anything to sell you a product that is out of your price range, this washer and dryer set has features that you don't need and probably will never use. This washer and dryer will fulfill your needs and offer much more than you expected, but so will the last one I showed you. To be honest, they both have the same 25 year warranty and they are both built to last. What you need to do is decide which one of these two would work best for you in your home." (*Here, you have done three things. You have brought to the consumers' attention the fact that salespeople will say anything to close a sale. You have also let them know that they had two products that fit their needs, but it was entirely up to them to decide which product would be best for them (In other words, there was ABSOLUTELY no pressure to make a purchase. Lastly, it was never mentioned that the least expensive product would fill their needs. I simply did not include this item because the customer requested certain features that the least expensive product did not have*).

People are easygoing and pleasant when you treat them with respect. While working in sales, you can "ARM" the consumer against the negative, pressure-laden tactics of less open-minded salespeople. You build trust, inform the consumer about the available products in an unbiased way, and respect their decisions. Even though you did not insist upon a sale, you can educate the consumer and make her feel that she is making the right decision based on the information you provided.

This is the beauty of my pressure-free method of selling. You never have to push to make a sale. You never have to feel guilty, and you enjoy the time you spend with the customer.

When you avoid pressure as a salesperson, you get the benefits of helping someone make an informed decision. This is what makes being a salesperson so enjoyable: working with the customer to reach the shared goal of finding the right item. Guiding customers away from those items that would not be good for them will leave them grateful towards you and eager to return to you when it is time to make another purchase. All customers can be compared to children who do not know the dangers that lurk around the corner. They must be protected, or (as I like to put it) "armed against harm." This is a big task with great rewards for those who are willing to take a chance.

YOU AS A CONSUMER

The next time you go shopping, take note of all the different methods salespeople use. It is entertaining to count how many different sales styles there really are. It seems as though there are as many different styles as there are salespeople. Since learning so much about sales through my experiences, I have found myself critiquing salespeople with my wife, and we enjoy laughing about what we see afterwards. One thing we have noticed about ourselves is that we like to deal with salespeople who left us feeling as if we'd had fun! Isn't that why we shop in the first place? An important part of shopping is enjoyment!

We can learn something from every salesperson out there. Whether it is a new tactic you can incorporate into your style or something that you would be better off avoiding, go out and have some fun with salespeople the next time you go on a shopping spree. You will be quite surprised at what you learn! Afterwards, it's a good idea to practice your pressure-free, ultra-courteous sales routine with someone so that you are ready for action when the time comes.

For Management

If you are working, or will be working in management, you have your work cut out for you! It is not easy to make the perfect decision for your company each and every time. Salespeople all have their own style and want to sell things in their own way. For the most part, this is okay, as long as they follow core company policies. I know that many managers take their jobs very seriously, and it is sometimes difficult to remember that work does not necessarily have to be hard. We all have many stressors in our everyday lives that we must handle on top of dealing with work-related challenges. As a manager, you have the power to create what I like to call "an escape from reality." Just because employees are having fun at work does not mean that they are not taking their work seriously. For employees who like what they do on the job, work can be a pleasant escape from the pressures of home life, and it is always an advantage to manage employees who enjoy their jobs. In many instances, the "reality" at home is not ideal for some employees, and deep down they come to work to get away from complications at home.

I would like you to look back to your younger years. Do you remember how time flew when you were having fun? While you were enjoying yourself as a kid, did you even notice how much energy you were exerting on an activity? Now, I'd like for you to remember a time when your parents took you to see or do something that was painstakingly boring. How did the time go by when you were loathing an experience? Do you remember how you knew exactly how much energy you were exerting and how much you wanted the event to be over? It makes sense that this same principle should work for grown-ups. If you create an environment where everyone can come and enjoy themselves, think about how much more productive everyone will be without even realizing it!

In order to create this type of environment, you have to be able to pinpoint and remove the "thorn" in the company's side (this "thorn" could be a person, policy, or procedure). Sometimes it can be blatantly obvious, and other times it can be a person you deeply trust. You have to be creative at times to figure out what obstacles are causing your company and staff problems. The first thing to do is perhaps the most difficult: you must take an impartial look at yourself and make sure that it is not you who is to blame. We tend to believe, in our minds, that we are flawless in every way. The truth is that no one is perfect.

For example, I once worked for a company where the manager thought very highly of himself. His staff was scared of giving him any input for fear of being fired or severely reprimanded. (*I personally do not do well in an environment where free speech is not welcome. I firmly believe we must constantly review and make changes to the way our company runs in order to allow it to grow and improve. This is also true with us as humans—we can always improve.*) At every sales meeting, the manager asked us to share our ideas and provide input on ways that the business could be improved. I spoke openly of ways the company could substantially learn from past situations I had previous experiences while working for a similar company, but every effort was cut down and tossed to the curb, so to speak.

Who wants to work hard in an environment where no one respects, considers, or even gives a second thought to the ideas of an associate? It is vitally important that everyone be given respect and feel like a part of something bigger than themselves. A successful business is one that changes with time and moves forward with new ideas from both employees and outside sources. The basic element of respect goes a long way in growing a successful, healthy business. (*Even if some ideas will perhaps prove impractical in the long run, the thought put into them should still be respected and encouragement should be offered for the input of additional ideas that will perhaps prove to be successful.*) Try some of the new ideas that are presented (*the ones that the majority of the **staff** believes may work*) and simply keep the ones that work and get rid of those that don't. Unfortunately, the company I was mentioning earlier failed to do this, and it is now having trouble staying in business. Because of one manager's close-minded attitude, the company is unable to move forward and is having financial problems.

Situations like this can be avoided if you show an open mind and do not take things personally. We, sometimes, have a tendency to exhibit a little jealousy when another employee has a good idea that we didn't think of ourselves. It is important to remember that there is no room for selfishness in a company. Competition shouldn't be so severe among employees that animosity develops when one employee has a particularly insightful idea. One should encourage these types of ideas as much as possible.

They make life for everyone easier in the long run! (*This includes—especially—the manager's!*). Everyone you work with may have their own ideas on how to improve their area of specialization. Not all ideas can be implemented, due to limitations of time and funding, but many can be. Those that cannot be used can be put on the shelf for later review and should not be forgotten or taken for granted. The employees in your workplace are the best source for new ideas on how to do things better. They have a thorough understanding of the inner workings of the company and of the details involved with their particular function in the workplace. Management should be constantly open to taking new ideas and implementing those that are likely to benefit the company.

The next step in improving the efficiency and productivity of a company or workplace, is to look at ALL of the sales staff and see which workers (if any) are holding the rest back (*emotionally*). For instance, consider a family. When one of your children acts up and causes everyone else grief, you naturally reprimand them. It should be the same with your work family. If an employee acts up, you must swiftly and decisively respond. This will instil in others a sense of the consequences that result from wrongful actions. However, it is important to keep consequences within reason. (*If an employee calls in sick at a time when it poses a significant hardship to the company for a worker to be missing, do not take your anger out on that employee. He or she may, in fact, be ill. You would only be justified in reprimanding him or her if sick days begin to occur frequently enough to arouse suspicion.*) In a family, when issues are beyond your own abilities to correct, it is acceptable or even necessary to seek outside help or counselling. Likewise, with your work family, you will sometimes need to hire outside help or consultants to get to the bottom of an issue. Everyone needs help at times in life, so you shouldn't feel like a failure if you find that it is necessary to resort to outside help. As I have said before, sometimes ideas come from within the company and sometimes they come from an outside source. It is through your own ability, perseverance, and knowledge that you know when to ask for help. This gives you strength. Realistically, does it really matter where the information comes from so long as you accomplish what you need to in the course of carrying out your job responsibilities?

One of the easiest ways to get to the bottom of an issue is to speak privately with your employees in a confidential setting. (*If an employee is causing a problem, it will usually become apparent through the matching accounts of several associates during this process. If attempts to rectify the situation prove unsuccessful, it could become necessary to remove the problem employee.*) If you have an open policy concerning manager-associate communication, then your employees should feel comfortable speaking with you about problems they see in the workplace. You might have to regain your employees' trust if you have been harsh with them in the past and have developed a reputation of an overbearing boss. Sometimes the best way to do this is by genuinely apologizing for past behavior and humbling yourself in front of your employees. (*This is very difficult for some managers, but it goes a long way in the eyes of your employees.*) This shows the staff that you are cognizant of the mistakes you have made, and your workers will see that you are mature enough to admit when you have done something unfair or inappropriate. In this way, you will open up communication channels and allow the "repair" process to begin between you and your employees. Whichever method you choose, remember that this process is not about "YOU." It is about the feelings and comfort of your staff and the kind of exchanges between you and your staff that will make your staff more productive. (As a general rule, *many of the sales tactics in this book can also be used to improve relations with your family members. Try it out and you will be surprised at the difference it can make.*)

On the whole, managers try very hard to make things work, but they can sometimes get "lost in the woods" as to what's going on in the minds of their workers. This can happen because some managers are already so far into the "forest" (*i.e., Too involved in micro-managing*) that they no longer see what changes will be most effective in re-establishing beneficial management practices. Remember that there is no right or wrong way—there is only the way that works best for your staff and your company's unique situation! Sometimes staying "out of the way" and letting events take their course is actually the best thing to do! Lighten up, be creative, and have fun!

SALES PROFIT

Traditionally, managers have been taught to maintain the highest margins possible in order to make the most money for the company. This may be a valid strategy from an accounting perspective but, in the real world, things are not as cut and dry as an accountant sees them.

I worked for a company that believed this method was the best way to maximize profits. They charged 15-20% more just because they felt their service and products were better. Although they made a lot of money at first, customers eventually began to stop purchasing from the company and sales became hard to close. This seemed odd to me so I took it upon myself to do some investigative work as to why customers were not making purchases at the same rate as before. The next time I did my follow-up calls and the consumer told me that they had made a purchase elsewhere, I asked them why they had decided to buy from our competitor. (*Because of my direct, non-evasive approach to selling, many consumers gave me the real reason they purchased elsewhere and it had nothing to do with my sales approach.*) I was surprised to discover that it was the cost of the products and services that was deterring customers. They did not see the value in spending 15-20% more when they could get the same product and service down the street for a lower price. Why do you think this happened?

Initially, consumers who purchased products from this company were very satisfied. (*There will sometimes be new customers that feel this way simply because they are not return customers.*) They would invite their friends over to show them their new purchase, but their friends would explain to them that, in fact, they may have overpaid for their new item. Customers would learn through their acquaintances that the same item was being sold by other companies at a cheaper price. The customer would be embarrassed and call other stores to find out if it was true that they were selling the same item for less money. Eventually, customers would end up angry at the company from whom they originally bought the product because they unknowingly overpaid because of this company's pricing system.

How many referrals do you think you would get from a customer who has been through this experience?

Of course a customer like this would never return for future business.

People tend to get excited when they have made a purchase, and they want to tell their friends about their new possession for various reasons. It's not always pride that makes people do this. Sometimes they are just genuinely excited about having the item, or often they desperately needed the item and they had told their friends about it before making the purchase. For all practical purposes, it really doesn't matter why they purchased the item. The important thing to keep in mind is that **people talk** about the purchases they make. This "word of mouth" publicity can be either detrimental or beneficial to a business. Is opting for a higher profit margin really worth more? Are you sure you aren't just being fooled by a policy that looks good on paper but ends up creating bad press for your company? By aiming for unrealistic profit margins, you can actually hurt your business. How? Let me give you two examples:

(Keep in mind that I am not saying with 100% certainty that higher margins are always more profitable on a per sale basis. From an accountant's perspective, it might appear that higher margins are more profitable on the surface of things. However, I will explain to you how it is not always more profitable in the long run when you take the "human factor" into consideration. Understand that there are ALWAYS people in the equation, and this one thing can save your business in the slow times.)

When a friend tells you, "Hey, I went to (?) and purchased a brand new (?). I only paid this much for it!" You will respond with what you know about the product and the retailers that sell similar products. If you know that your friend's new item is sold elsewhere for less money, you'll be likely to respond, "Wow that's awesome, but I think you overpaid." Your friend will quickly realize that he or she was overcharged, and he or she will probably be eager to spread the word that the store where the purchase was made is likely to be overcharging on a variety of items. And yourself? Do you think that you would buy from a store where your friend was overcharged? It's pretty unlikely.

How do you think it would affect your decision if your friend said "I went to (?) and they were really helpful and knowledgeable. Their prices were not the cheapest, but their service was fantastic and the product looks great! You should check out this store!"

As you can see from the first example, what you create by encouraging the high margin mentality is a onetime customer without referrals. Is this what a company really wants? Is this going to bring a company real, lasting success? This method might work in a thriving economy, but in a market where consumers are shrewd and constantly trying to save money, the results will not be good. The second scenario—high prices but excellent service—raises your chances of keeping current clients as well as acquiring more clients, which in turn equates to continued profits! It is common sense, really. But, when companies can only see dollar signs, they tend to forget that they are dealing with real people who are constantly comparing information about prices and shopping experiences amongst themselves.

People Talk!

What do you want them to be saying about your business?

Try to use this common sense method of strategy development when deciding on things that affect your business. Consumers will go where their friends went, only if their friends were pleased with the overall shopping experience. The beautiful thing about referred customers is that they have already been pre-sold on your products and/or service. Word of mouth is the best form of advertising, and it is absolutely free! Be smart, and remember that salespeople and companies depend on referrals to succeed.

I was fortunate enough to realize this on my own and implement it early on in my career. My customers would refer their friends to me on a regular basis. Eventually, I could not handle all of the work that was coming in, and others in the company had to help to handle all of the new clients. Other employees could see my success and followed my example. Many of the sales staff began asking me questions regarding my method. They started using the method I showed them and tailored it to their own personal style. How much do you think your profits would increase if you started using this method?

In-Store Marketing Techniques

- Have you ever gone into a store and seen sales tags on every item?
- How is it possible that every item in the store is on sale?
- Doesn't having every item on sale defeat the purpose of having a sale to begin with?

The purpose of putting something on sale is to make it stand out. In a sea of sale items, the only thing that stands out is the items that aren't on sale. What I am trying to get at is this: If you tag every item on sale, nothing stands out and the sale has no effect. It is better to put only a few items on sale at a time, and then change the sale items from time to time to give some variety. If everything in the store is truly on sale, then use a different color on items you really want to feature. Develop some clever techniques to make featured items really stand out in the eyes of the customers who walk into your store.

Imagine a newspaper page full of writing. Take one 2" x 2" square from the middle of the page and leave it blank. This is where the eye will be drawn, because this part of the page is different and stands out. Use this same concept with your sales tags. It is simple but very effective.

This brings me to the five "**methods of perception.**" These methods of perception are our five senses:

- Smell
- Touch
- Taste
- Sight
- Sound

As humans, we judge things before we realize we are even making judgements. We judge things by the way they make us feel. This tendency is not the first sense we use, but it is a response generated by all of our senses working together in unison when we initially contemplate a new item, idea, or situation. When we smell popcorn, for instance, it gives us a certain feeling that is generally associated with a memory. For me, it calls to mind going to the ice skating arena as a child. For you, the smell of popcorn could bring back a good, bad, or neutral memory. But it's the feeling we are trying to focus on here:

What makes you feel good, happy, or excited?

Now think about the general public and what your particular clientele will have in common. The next time you go into your store, office, or workplace, I'd like you to stop before you enter and . . . feel . . . as you walk in the front door. I'd like you to focus on each individual sense. You will be astonished by the things you feel and the immediate changes you want to make.

I once knew a business owner who had beautiful plastic potted plants in his showroom. Once a week, he would change the soil in his plants. You might ask why he would change the soil for plastic plants. He was putting fresh ground coffee in the potted plants so his store would smell like coffee. He in fact had a nice coffee station to the right of the door when you walked into his showroom, and he made it look like he actually made coffee to drink at this station. His business flourished and people always commented on how they loved coming into his store because of the fresh coffee smell. It is such a small detail, but it made other people talk about the store in a positive way.

What is the first thing you do when you wake up in the morning? Do you make coffee? That is what this business owner did. He knew that by having such a common, recognizable smell in his showroom, customers would be reminded of his store when they made coffee at home in the morning. This is really an incredibly clever way to attract business. What can you do for your customers in a similar way to draw people into your store? We all become complacent over time and stop noticing things because we are wrapped up in the everyday tasks and the mundane details of our job responsibilities. Sometimes it is these simple things like the smell of coffee that can make a salesperson or business more successful than the competition. Really take some time to consider this and see what you can come up with . . . you will be surprised by how many people notice even the simplest changes in your sales environment.

Conclusion

I want to take a moment to thank you for putting the time into learning some new things or maybe brushing up on things you already knew about. Salespeople, Managers, Owners. We are all the same. We are all trying to make a living the best way we know how. We all want to find happiness in some way. Perhaps we want to be the richest person in the world, find the love of our lives, be green . . . whatever the case may be, I wish you all the best in life's journey. Don't let fear of success stand in your way as it did for me for many years. If you are great, tell the world about it and show them that there is nothing you can't accomplish if you set your mind to it. The only person holding you back is you!

Good luck!